tom catalano

Copyright © 2023 by Thomas E. Catalano

*To Peggy, who laughs at (almost) all
of my funny poems and who
supports me unconditionally.*

*Back cover photo:
Emma Louise Photography
@emmalouisemoments*

**All rights reserved. No part of this work may
be reproduced or transmitted in any form
or by any means, electronic or mechanical,
including photocopying, recording, or by any
information storage and retrieval system or
used in any form without written permission
from the author.**

ISBN 978-1-882646-13-5

Published by:
Wordsmith Books
P.O. Box 1608, Crossville, TN 38558 USA
tomcatalano.com

CONTENTS

I. Life Is A Journey...Bring A Map!

The First Thing To Go 7

Productive 8

At That Age 9

My Bags Have Bags! 10

I'm Growing! 11

Getting Older 12

Snap, Crackle, Pop 13

So Tired 14

Ooh My Back! 15

Lazy 16

I Can't Sleep 17

I Forgot 18

I'm Busy 19

In A Good Mood 20

Pendulum 21

II. The Funny Side Of Love And Friendship

Squirrelly 22

No Secrets 23

Hot & Cold 24

Baby Announcement 26

The Honey-Do List 27

● ● ●

My GPS 28

The Fridge Calendar 29

Ramble On 30

Leave Your Name and Number 31

My Friends 32

The Nasty Neighbors 34

III. The Quirky Side Of Life

Sally's Single Shingles Shot 35

Before Technology 36

We've Been Trying To Reach You 37

We Lost Power! 38

My Brain's Not A Computer 40

I Think I Can, I Think I Can 41

Time To Buy A Car 42

The Impending Bug Uprising 44

IV. Fine, If You Can Find The Time

Retired 45

How To Win At Solitaire 46

Quilter's Lingo 47

Fishing Is Not Easy 48

Fishing Wishing 49

The Year Of The Tomatoes 50

My Blockbuster 53

V. Things Don't Always Go As Expected

Desire For The Choir 58

Stink Breath 60

This Poem Stinks 62

I Took A Dump Truck 64

Life Coach 66

A Blink And A Wink 68

VI. Scrambled Thoughts, Over Easy

Willie The Wheelbarrow 70

Pert Near Impossible 71

The Poem Request 72

I'll Write My Own Prescription 74

A Thinking Drink 75

I Know Me 76

The Replenisher 77

What I Must Have 78

VII. 'Tis The Season, That's The Reason

The Year Of The Cicadas 79

My Staycation 80

Autumn Leaves 82

Halloween 83

Santa's Retirement 84

OTHER BOOKS by Tom Catalano 89

The First Thing To Go

They say that the mind

is the FIRST thing to go

    and memories you start to miss.

My mind is as sharp

as it EVER was and,

    umm…where was I going with this?

tom catalano

Productive

Today I am determined

    to not procrastinate.

I will not put off little things

    that I dislike or hate.

I WILL be most productive

    with no regrets or sorrow.

I can't WAIT to get things done

    — I'll start FIRST THING TOMORROW!

tom catalano

At That Age

I am at that age,

    maybe you are too.

Every day I have a goal

    — something I should do.

Only ONE because

    then I have to rest.

It's just I know my body

    — it is for the best.

Maybe I will rake,

    maybe I will mow,

maybe to the grocery store

    I will choose to go.

Have another chore?

    I just can't, no way.

For you see, I wrote this rhyme

    — I am DONE today!

tom catalano

My Bags Have Bags!

I am getting older

  this is no surprise,

and I have gotten bags

  under both my eyes.

But now my bags have bags

  — when's it gonna stop,

after I get bags on

  the sides and on the top?!

IF I get more puffy

  I'll be a different fellow

and I will look just like

  a big ol' fat marshmallow!

tom catalano

I'm Growing!

I've noticed something strange with me,

I've stopped growing vertically.

Now the thing that I can see,

I'm growing HORIZONTALLY!

tom catalano

Getting Older

I know I'm getting older
    and wrinkles I can see,
but that is not the only change
    happening to me.
I find I'm much more jiggly
    than ever was before,
and I can still bend over
    but I can't touch the floor.
And sometimes I forget what
    it was that I just said,
or I can't find my glasses
    still sitting on my head.
But I remember lots of friends
    and what they mean to me.
All the ones who make me smile
    and those I like to see.
And I can even still recall
    how I got to know 'em.
But I just can't remember
    why I wrote this po-em!

tom catalano

Snap, Crackle, Pop

I wake up in the morning

    and my bones begin to crack.

My tendons start to pop

    and my knees begin to snap.

I'm sounding like Rice Krispies

    and I wish that it would stop.

I guess I'm getting old cuz

    I snap, and crackle, pop!

tom catalano

So Tired

I watch TV, it's late at night

    and just like that — out like a light.

I'll go to bed — a big mistake,

    cuz there I lie — wide awake.

So I get up and watch TV,

    doesn't matter what I see.

My eyelids droop and no surprise,

    I do not sleep, just rest my eyes.

But just like that I lose the fight

    and once again — out like a light.

So back to bed a nap I'll take,

    but once again I'm wide awake.

I'm so tired I could weep.

    I only wish that I could sleep!

tom catalano

Ooh My Back!

I did some chores outside

    and then I hurt my back.

Don't know how it happened

    but now it's out of whack.

I'll have to take it easy,

    reduce my pain and strife.

If there're any chores to do

    I'll leave them for my wife!

tom catalano

Lazy

I wish I had more energy,

I'm lazy as can be.

I'd like to finish this poem, but…

…see?

tom catalano

I Can't Sleep

I lay in bed and think about
what I'm going to wear,
where I'm going to go today
and how I will get there.

I make a list of what to buy
at the grocery store.
I wonder if I'll have the time
to finish every chore.

I wonder if I clean the house
what I'd toss or keep.
All this while I'm lying here
— no wonder I can't sleep!

tom catalano

I Forgot

I remember…no, I don't,

   the thought just went away.

I can't for the life of me

   remember what to say.

I'm sure it was important,

   and something I should share.

Now it's gone and I can't think

   of why I thought you'd care.

But I can't go back doing

   what I did because

I just can't remember

   whatever that it was!

tom catalano

I'm Busy

I'm busy doing nothing

    as you can plainly see.

I can't be interrupted

    — and that's just FINE with me.

I'm busy doing nothing,

    it might just take all day.

I'm thinking that tomorrow

    just might be the SAME WAY.

tom catalano

In A Good Mood

I'm in a good mood

    — I know, a surprise.

There's nothing I hate,

    regret, or despise.

Do me a favor

    and don't laugh or scoff.

Whatever you do,

    please, don't piss me off!

tom catalano

Pendulum

Some people call me 'Pendulum,'

of this I don't dispute.

Some days I may just care a lot

or I don't give a hoot.

My opinion it may vary

— depends on time of day.

If you should ask me what I think,

you don't know what I'll say.

They say I'm unpredictable,

but that is just a lie.

They may not know what I'll say next

— but frankly, nor do I.

tom catalano

Squirrelly

She's a squirrelly girly

    but what else can she be?

It takes a squirrelly girly

    to like a squirrelly me!

tom catalano

No Secrets

I don't want that there should be

any secrets 'tween you and me.

Let's share it all from bad to worst.

So don't hold back — YOU go first.

tom catalano

Hot & Cold

My wife runs hot

    and I run cold.

This is normal,

    I am told.

When she wears shorts

    I wear a sweater.

She feels good and

    I feel better.

We don't argue

    on this or that,

except who sets

    the thermostat.

"Make it cooler,"

    she will say,

"or I may just

    melt away." ● ● ●

I start to plead,

    "Turn up the heat.

I can't even

    feel my feet!"

She likes the snow,

    I like the beach.

A compromise

    we must reach.

So for vacation

    we agree,

we stay home and

    watch TV!

tom catalano

Baby Announcement

There's crying at our house again

with big ol' jumbo tears.

There's all that waking up at night

with lots of unknown fears.

There's ranting and there's raving,

it's SO painful to see.

Oh, the baby is just fine

— the crying is from ME!

tom catalano

The Honey-Do List

It's no surprise but I've got news.

I've got a list of 'honey-do's.'

Go mow the grass and paint the shed,

clean the gutters, make the bed.

Wash the dishes — that's not all.

Get that spider on the wall.

Just when I think that I am done,

it's "Honey, here's another one!"

tom catalano

My GPS

I really don't need GPS

    when driving in my car.

I have no trouble getting there

    whether near or far.

And I never use a map

    it sounds so strange, I know.

My wife is more than happy to

    tell me where to go!

tom catalano

The Fridge Calendar

We have got so much to do

it seems like every day.

We have to keep it organized

and we have found a way.

A calendar's not large enough,

it's too small by a smidge.

Instead, we post the things to do

taped upon the fridge!

tom catalano

Ramble On

I don't have too much to say

    and my wife likes it that way.

For in the past I have rambled,

    my thoughts were all a little scrambled.

I'd spew out thoughts left and right,

    sometimes late into the night.

She rolls her eyes and just says, "Wow,"

    when I ramble on — like NOW.

tom catalano

Leave Your Name And Number

It's not that I hate people,

that simply isn't true.

I often get along with me,

and sometimes even you.

It is just that I prefer

that I be left alone.

So if you want to talk to me

try calling on the phone.

Of course, I will not answer,

not even if it's you.

So please don't be offended cuz

THIS you already knew.

tom catalano

My Friends

I turned around the corner
   and I saw my buddy, Sam.
He did not see me coming
   and I hit him with my van.
Sam fell down upon the ground
   and then he hit his head.
I tried to help him, but too late,
   and now poor Sam is dead.

I took a ride upon my boat
   so Bill, my friend, could ski.
BUT I must have turned too fast —
   his line I did not see.
He yelled to me, I did not know,
   and next thing he went down.
I tried to help him, but too late,
   and that is how Bill drowned. ● ● ●

At the diner that I went

    I saw my buddy, Joe.

He said he liked the spicy food

    and this I did not know.

I asked the chef to make him

    some chili, extra hot.

One mouthful did him in cuz he's

    allergic and forgot.

I don't know why it's like this,

    it's really a surprise.

But every time I make a friend

    they seem to drop like flies.

tom catalano

The Nasty Neighbors

The moving truck was rolling

    and it was moving slow.

There weren't any tear-filled eyes

    — we were glad to see them go.

They were mean and spiteful

    the whole time they were here.

They'd complain to management

    every little thing they'd hear.

We may never meet again

    though one can never tell.

If we don't live a righteous life

    then we may meet in…well,

I guess we will not meet again

    and that would be okay.

I'll just stand here waving,

    relieved they went away.

tom catalano

Sally's Single Shingles Shot

Sally got a shingles shot,

    her shoulder stiff and sore.

It was just a single shot,

    she'd have to get one more.

So Saturday sad Sally went,

    a second shot she'd do.

Afterwards she found out that

    she'd need one for the flu!

tom catalano

Before Technology

Our parents were so brave

    when they went out alone.

They did not have a GPS

    and did not have a phone.

But things are different now,

    I'm sure of this you know.

If I don't have my phone with me

    I just as soon not go!

tom catalano

We've Been Trying To Reach You

I am very worried

for I just got a call.

Yes, this was a surprise

— not expecting it at all.

They sounded so concerned,

I don't know what to do.

My car's extended warranty

has lapsed, I must renew!

If you ask me, it sounds strange

and a little bit bizarre,

why I need a warranty

— I don't even own a car!

tom catalano

We Lost Power!

A storm came up, the lights went out,
    and we are without power.
How could this be? We cannot see
    at this ungodly hour.

Where's the candle?! Where's the flashlight?!
    Ouch! I kicked the table!
I'd like to try and call for help
    if only I was able!

Computer's off, TV don't work,
    and I can't find the phone!
The fridge is off, the food will spoil
    and we will starve alone! • • •

They'll find our bones all shriveled up,

the house all cold and black...!!

(PAUSE)

Oh, never mind what I just said,

the power just came back.

tom catalano

My Brain's Not A Computer

Thinking's overrated

    I don't care what they say.

I'm so tired of thinking

    each and every day.

My brain's not a computer,

    now THAT would be a treat.

Every thought that I don't like

    I would hit 'delete.'

I'd UPload some new data,

    yes THAT would be a hoot.

And any time I get confused

    I would just reboot!

My brain's not a computer

    and frankly it's not fair.

I'm afraid I would find out

    it's OPERATOR ERROR!

tom catalano

I Think I Can,
I Think I Can

When tackling a project,

    I am optimistic.

I always want to jump right in

    and see if I can fix it.

I'm like the little engine

    that's heading up the hill,

"I think I can, I think I can,"

    and tackle it I will.

BUT it never goes as planned,

    instead, I tend to fail.

That stupid little engine

    it slides right off the rail!

tom catalano

Time To Buy A Car

I think the time has come

   for me to buy a car.

I guess that I am lazy

   — don't want to walk too far.

I checked out all the ads

   and went down to the lot.

I don't have much money,

   but let's see what they got.

The sales guy who met me,

   he said that I could trust

he had the perfect car

   that didn't have much rust.

The seats they all had holes,

   the headlights wouldn't light,

I'd have to drive in day

   — I COULDN'T drive at night.   • • •

He said that it would start

    but the battery was dead.

The tires they were bald,

    and here is what he said:

"The car's a real gem

    and you can have it cheap.

What's it gonna take to

    put you in the seat?"

While it's true I need a car,

    and I admit I'm lazy,

but I think that I will pass

    — I sure as HECK ain't crazy!

tom catalano

The Impending Bug Uprising

I've heard it said there are more bugs

    than people on the planet.

If that's true, I don't think we

    should take the world for granted.

Heaven help if they decide

    to catch us by surprise.

The ants and bugs and critters

    could gather and uprise.

Let's face it, they already try

    to get into our home.

Don't turn your back on a bug

    and NEVER be alone!

tom catalano

Retired

I no longer punch a clock

but I am still quite busy.

I've so many projects that

it makes my head go dizzy.

I shovel snow in winter,

I rake the leaves in fall.

I mow the grass in summer,

and brother, that's not all.

I've lots of household projects

just as you'd think I might.

I start in early morning

and don't stop 'til the night.

I know that it is sounding

like I'm some sort of snob,

but I am working harder NOW

than when I had a job!

tom catalano

How To Win At Solitaire

Here I sit upon my chair

    playing games of solitaire.

They make me smile, make me grin,

    at these games I always win.

Here's the secret, here's the clue,

    I will share this hint with you.

If you don't wish to face defeat,

    just do what I do — cheat!

tom catalano

Quilter's Lingo

My wife she is a quilter,

    a talent I can't match.

I'VE learned what a 'bobbin' is

    and something called '9-patch.'

She said she needed 'batting'

    — yes, most good players do.

"Let's go to the batting cage,

    I'D like to hit a few!"

When she mentions 'jellyroll'

    or talks of 'layer cake,'

it always makes me hungry

    and lunch I have to make.

Quilting is a different thing

    — a language most unique.

I guess I'd better learn some more

    BEFORE I try to speak!

tom catalano

Fishing Is Not Easy

Fishing is my hobby
    it's how I pass the time.
I'm drawn to the water
    and then throw out a line.
Will I catch a marlin?
    Perhaps a rainbow trout?
Or land a big old muskie?
    That's what it's all about.
Land a couple dozen
    and fry 'em in the pan,
have a hearty dinner
    — at least that is the plan.
But fishing is not easy
    despite what you've been told.
I may not catch a fish but
    I ALWAYS catch a cold!

tom catalano

Fishing Wishing

Man, I caught a big one,

fishing at the lake.

Not to sound ungrateful, but

I wish it was a steak.

tom catalano

The Year Of The Tomatoes

This year, I grew tomatoes

that I started in the yard.

I just spread some seeds around,

it wasn't very hard.

In just a little while

some plants began to sprout.

Maybe I'll get tomatoes

— what the effort's all about.

The plants they started growing,

not just SOME but ALL.

There were so MANY of them,

they all grew big and tall. ●●●

Tomatoes started blooming,

    but just a few at first.

A couple for a salad

    — that wouldn't be the worst.

But many more did grow,

    they ripened on the vine.

And once I started picking,

    I was picking all the time!

At first I filled a basket

    and then I soon filled TWO.

When I filled a dozen more

    I knew not what to do.

My table, it was covered,

    as was my countertop.

And still the plants kept growing,

    when will this bounty stop?! ● ● ●

I went and made spaghetti sauce

and made some chili too.

Even filled my freezer up,

WHAT else could I do?

I gave some to the neighbors,

but they said, "Please, no more.

Stop leaving these tomatoes

on the step outside our door!"

Tomatoes they kept growing,

my house is overrun.

Now I have to wonder

what it is that I've begun.

But now I've learned a lesson

and my neighbors I won't feed 'em.

WHEN I want tomatoes

I'll BUY 'em if I need 'em!

tom catalano

My Blockbuster

I sit and write my stories
    because it's what I know.
Like Steinbeck, Lewis, Hemingway,
    or Edgar Allan Poe.

The plot unfurls from my mind
    down to my fingertips.
I have to stop and read out loud
    like nectar from my lips.

The characters all took form,
    I made it look so easy.
Some of them were quite demure
    and some of them were sleazy.

Adventures that I sent them on
    they went so willingly.
I wondered, was I leading THEM
    or were they leading ME?   •••

No matter, cuz the story
      was a brilliant work of art.
To think that only YESTERDAY
      I wondered where to start.

But start this masterpiece I did,
      and FINISH it as well.
There was just ONE thing left to do,
      the world I would tell.

"What an epic story,
      we love what it's about!
The greatest author of our time!"
      I hoped that they would shout.

I knew that I'd be humble
      in spite of accolades.
Like interviewing on TV
      and ticker-tape parades. ● ● ●

I found a big shot agent
    so they could pitch my tale.
I knew that with their backing
    no way that I could fail.

In only three days passing
    that agent sent a note.
I had to sit and take a breath
    for here is what they wrote:

"Thanks so much for reaching out,
    I appreciate your time.
Unfortunately, I must
    respectfully decline."

Sad and disappointed,
    I'll trip but I won't fall.
And I was ready for the next
    solicitation call.   ● ● ●

When begging for donations
    or extended warranty,
I went and made them sorry
    that they ever messed with ME.

I said, "Thanks for reaching out,
    I appreciate your time.
Unfortunately, I must
    respectfully decline."

Just by venting out this way
    it made me feel better.
That is, until the mail came,
    — an I.R.S. tax letter.

They wrote I had a problem,
    and said they don't agree
that an unpublished novel
    presents a LOSS to me.   • • •

They said I owed them tax,
    a quite substantial sum.
So I wrote them back this note
    just to have some fun:

"Thanks so much for reaching out,
    I appreciate your time.
Unfortunately, I must
    respectfully decline."

Now I sit inside my cell
    no accolades or glory,
planning out the storyline
    of my NEXT blockbuster story!

tom catalano

Desire For The Choir

It's been my heart's desire
    to join the church's choir.
They were looking for some men
    — I prayed, and said, "Amen!"

I went to the audition
    and then took my position.
Director said, "Begin,"
    and so I jumped right in.

So I was feeling proud,
    I belted it out loud.
Knowing what they're after
    I shouted to the rafter.

Director raised his hand
    and said, "I understand
it is your heart's desire
    to join the church's choir.   • • •

We need somebody soon,

    but YOU can't hold a tune!"

Ouch, this I can't believe,

    and so I had to leave.

There's ONE thing I can say,

    I wasn't good that day.

But IT won't make me sour,

    I sound GREAT in the shower!

tom catalano

Stink Breath
(or Your Honor, I Had No Choice)

Your honor, I just had no choice,
I tried to solve it with my voice.

But there was nothing I could say
to make this person go away.

I admit it wasn't right,
what I did that awful night.

But they drove me raving mad
because of food they must have had.

Their breath, your honor, it was rank
and when they talked it really stank.

Garlic, pepper, I don't know,
I just wanted them to go.

There is one thing I am sure —
their breath, it smelled like horse manure. ● ● ●

Your honor, every time they spoke
it really made me want to choke.

I tried leaving but no way,
they always had something to say.

Your honor, I could take no more,
so I knocked them to the floor.

What I did it wasn't right,
but I'd been breathing stink all night.

They didn't even get the hint
when I offered them a mint.

I know that what I did was bad
but stink breath, well, it drove me mad.

I know I must sound like a nut —
they should have kept their stink mouth shut.

If you throw the book, oh well.
But I won't soon forget that smell!

tom catalano

This Poem Stinks

There was a man down at the zoo

    who had a job no one would do.

He didn't know just what they meant

    — they said he'd be in excrement.

He knew in order to succeed

    he'd have to clean or have to feed,

but on his first day he would find

    while trainers trained, he walked behind.

He'd follow every elephant

    and sweep up everywhere they went.

One day a pachyderm did bind

    and nothing came from its behind.

A trainer handed him a hose,

    "Just stand back if there she blows."

The figs and prunes just didn't work,

    so the hose went in — with a jerk.

Suddenly, before he knew,

    a low and distant rumble grew.   ● ● ●

An avalanche came tumbling down

    and knocked the man down to the ground.

Two hundred pounds fell on his head

    and when they found him he was dead.

His wife found out and then she cried,

    "He took some crap at work and died!"

We KNOW what this poem's all about

    — what goes in MUST come out!

tom catalano

I Took A Dump Truck

I took a dump truck for a ride,
    I'd never driven one.
I took that dump truck for a spin,
    I thought that it'd be fun.

I thought that trying something new
    was well within my right.
But they don't like it when it's from
    a live construction site.

I guess I should have known it though,
    the truck was filled with rocks.
The truck was hard for me to steer,
    I went just a FEW blocks.

The truck was hard to handle as
    I drove it down the road.
And so I pushed a button and
    I dropped the heavy load.

● ● ●

In hindsight, that was not too smart,
    I wouldn't get too far,
for I had dropped that heavy load
    right on a passing car.

And now I'm sitting in a cell,
    and I've come to decide,
I don't think that it's smart to take
    a dump truck for a ride.

tom catalano

Life Coach

I wish I had a life coach
    to help me as I go,
cuz frankly, there're a lot of things
    that I just do not know.

Someone to advise me
    if I could do things better,
like making conversation
    or how to write a letter.

They'd follow and observe
    explaining as we go,
why I do the things I do
    and things I ought to know.   ● ● ●

They would be my shadow and

WITH me through the day,

giving me suggestions

of what to do or say.

They would follow me around

until I'm getting sleepy.

Uh oh, wait, on second thought,

that's a little creepy.

tom catalano

A Blink And A Wink

A speck of dirt flew in my eye
I couldn't see a thing.
I tried to rub it but no luck,
it only made it sting.

It started then to water
which only made me blink.
A woman standing near me
thought it was a wink.

She stepped a little closer,
my good eye I could see.
She smiled and said, "I noticed
the wink you gave to me."

I knew I was in trouble
but knew not what to do.
She said, "Although I'm flattered,
it wouldn't work with you. ● ● ●

My husband he is jealous,

    it's something you should know.

So we should fight temptation,

    you'll have to let me go."

I hardly knew what I should do,

    so I just said, "Goodbye."

All this because a speck of dirt

    got stuck into my eye.

tom catalano

Willie The Wheelbarrow

I have a wheelbarrow
    I love to call "Drunk Willie."
I know it doesn't need a name,
    but I was feeling silly.

Drunk Willie's always ready,
    for any kind of task.
Why is he "Drunk Willie"?
    Well, funny you should ask.

I can always count on him,
    hardworking, but moreover,
if he gets too loaded up
    poor Willie falls right over!

tom catalano

Pert Near Impossible

It's pert near impossible
 to rhyme a word like 'pert.'
Unless the rhyming word I choose
 to rhyme with 'pert' is 'shirt.'

I suppose that 'hurt' would work,
 so would 'alert' and 'dirt.'
I guess it's NOT impossible
 to rhyme a word like 'pert.'

I am guessing I would have
 a much, much, harder time,
if the word was 'orange.'
 Yeah, good luck with THAT rhyme!

tom catalano

The Poem Request

I got asked to write a poem,
    but I just walked away.
Do they think it's easy to
    find rhyming words to say?

I agreed to write a poem,
    I guess I felt I should.
They lost a family member,
    I want it to be good.

They loved this family member
    more than any other.
They were very special,
    like a sister or a brother.

They want a special message
    to tell the world that
the world is a sadder place
    because they lost their cat. • • •

I sat down at the table
    and this is what I said:
"I hope you're fine all the time
    — guess what? My cat is dead!"

They said they did not like it
    and want another try.
Just something sentimental
    that makes you want to cry.

I sat back at the table
    determined not to rush it.
"Fluffy died, and so we cried.
    Too bad we couldn't flush it."

They're not speaking to me,
    I guess that it's okay,
cuz I really didn't want
    to write one anyway.

tom catalano

I'll Write My Own Prescription

I went to see the doctor

    because I had an ache.

I wanted her to take a look

    and to investigate.

It wasn't very serious,

    and it should go away.

There's nothing else that she can do

    to help me out today.

I'll write my own prescription

    — I'll have a glass of wine.

It WILL not cure what ails me

    but I will feel fine.

If it isn't better

    I know what I might do.

If a glass of wine works well

    then maybe I'll have TWO!

tom catalano

A Thinking Drink

Coffee is a thinking drink,
I think I'll have some more.
I think I may be running low,
I think I'll buy some more.
I think I like it chilled,
I think that it is fine.
Coffee is a thinking drink
but then again…so's WINE!

tom catalano

I Know Me

If you ask me, I know me.

    I've known me all my life.

I've known me longer than my friends

    and longer than my wife.

I'm not right ALL of the time,

    sometimes I disagree.

Sometimes I have an argument

    and get upset at me.

I may go for days on end

    pretending I'm not there.

If something GOOD does happen,

    I pretend that I don't care.

I CAN'T stay mad forever,

    it's just too hard, you see,

to stay upset at someone who

    I've known as long as me.

tom catalano

The Replenisher

They call me 'The Replenisher'

— they all depend on me.

When things are almost empty

no one seems to see.

The paper towels or napkins

are empty as can be.

Who's the one who fills 'em up?

You guessed it, it is me.

Replenishing these products

it doesn't bother me.

But if you wouldn't mind too much

— replace the darn TP!

tom catalano

What I Must Have

There're just a couple of things
I MUST have in my life.
I know what you are thinking,
and no, it's not my wife.

A television screen
that's 60 inch or larger.
Not to mention my cell phone
AND of course, the charger.

These are just the things I need
to make me feel fine.
And, perhaps, another thing
— a bottle of good wine!

tom catalano

The Year Of The Cicadas

Oh those darn cicadas

with buzzing in my ear.

I see them flying overhead

— their shells are everywhere.

I don't really blame them

that they are all around,

but I wish that they'd go back

to somewhere underground!

tom catalano

My Staycation

I'm going on staycation
    and I will go alone.
It's much like a vacation,
    but I will stay at home.

I have seen the 'sights' before,
    there's really no surprise.
There are NO angry locals
    or foods that I despise.

The bed is nice and comfy,
    the coffee piping hot.
You may think it's boring,
    believe me, no it's not. ● ● ●

Maybe I will read a book

or I'll go on a hike.

Maybe I will play some golf

or I may ride a bike.

I'll watch a favorite movie

or maybe have a beer.

My favorite destination

is when I stay right HERE!

tom catalano

Autumn Leaves

The autumn leaves are falling,

mosaic on the ground,

like shards of broken rainbow

spread littered all around.

For some, a favorite season,

to each his own, I guess.

But some of us are raking

and cleaning up this mess!

tom catalano

Halloween

I do not know what happened,
  perhaps it was the rain.
But here it is on Halloween
  and not one child came.

I bought all of this candy
  down at the grocery store.
I put it in a bowl and
  then set it by the door.

The time for trick-or-treaters
  it came and then it went,
and I was left remembering
  all the money spent.

Instead of getting angry,
  instead of being sad,
I think I'll eat it all myself
  which doesn't sound too bad!

tom catalano

Santa's Retirement

The trips, they all seemed longer,
    and he was getting tired.
He told his wife that maybe
    it's time that he retired.

Yes, he delivered presents
    like a good old elf would do,
but now he started thinking
    after all these years he's through.

The aches and pains were plenty,
    lifting bags into the sleigh.
A tooth might have a cavity,
    his feet hurt every day.

The things around the house
    were needing some repair.
But they had gone neglected
    cuz he was hardly there. •••

The leaky kitchen faucet,
 the broken window shutter,
the squeaky basement stairway,
 the leaves stuck in the gutter.

The drafty bedroom window,
 all the bathroom tile grout,
the garage that's filled with junk
 all needing to throw out.

The roof it needs a shingle,
 and the carpet it is worn,
the house could use a painting,
 the curtains they are torn.

The sleigh could use new runners,
 and a lot of other stuff.
All this will take a lifetime
 — should he live LONG enough! •••

He'll postpone retirement,

those household chores he'll shirk.

Flying all around the world

just sounds like much less work!

tom catalano

OTHER BOOKS by Tom Catalano:

- **Rhyme & Reason**
  The author's first rhyming book. A wide range of subjects and emotions. Many funny poems. Chapters on Christmas, love, nature, and more. Includes: *A Child's Christmas, Work Dreams, Las Vegas Vacation of Mine, Wanderlust,* and *Pearanoid.* 96 pgs. Adult & teen. (ISBN 978-1-882646-07-4)

- **Poetry 'N Motion**
  Rhyming poems to make you laugh and feel good. Includes poems on Christmas, family, love, and more. Favorites include *I Got A Pain, Golfer's Lament, Beside Me All The Way,* and *The Innkeeper.* 96 pgs. Adult & teen. (ISBN 978-1-882646-03-6)

- **Verse Things First**
  Fun rhyming poems to tickle your funny bone or have you feeling sentimental. Includes *Coffee Crutch, Family Tree, This Kitchen, For You, Mai-Tai's, The Mission,* and more. Many poems about Christmas. 96 pgs. Adult & teen. (ISBN 978-1-882646-43-2)

More books on next page!

OTHER BOOKS by Tom Catalano:

- **Poems For His Glory**
  Expect to feel God's presence while reading these faith-inspiring rhyming poems (i.e. *Hope, Heaven, A Cross To Bear, Repaid*). Many positive reviews by faith leaders of various religious denominations. Co-written by Emma Catalano. 96 pgs, paperback. All ages. (ISBN 978-1-882646-09-8)

- **I Dig Mud & Yellow Blood**
  Funny and touching rhyming poems about Caterpillar, Inc. (the heavy equipment manufacturer), CAT dealers, and the people who use construction equipment. Anyone familiar with Caterpillar will enjoy this! 48 pgs, paperback. Adult & teen. (ISBN 978-1-882646-91-3)

- **Witty Words of Wisdom**
  150 original funny, clever, inspiring, and thought-provoking nuggets of wit and wisdom. Samples: *"I'm not lazy, I'm selectively productive." "Getting older is just nature's way of seasoning to taste." "I did not grow up, I was raised."* 96 pgs, paperback. Adult & teen. (ISBN 978-1-882646-11-1)

OTHER BOOKS by Tom Catalano:

- **Nicholas, The Santa Story**
  The rhyming story of how Nicholas chose to become Santa after hearing the voice of God and visiting Baby Jesus. An original heartwarming story that connects the birth of Jesus with the secular traditions of the holiday. Very popular with children, parents, and grandparents. 44 pgs, hardcover, illustrated. All ages. (ISBN 978-1-882646-12-8)

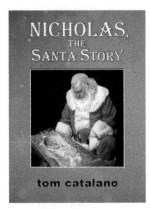

- **The Edge of Imagination**
  Eleven short stories of urban science fiction and psychological suspense. Ordinary people put in extraordinary situations with surprise endings. If you like the *Twilight Zone* TV show, you'll love these stories! 176 pgs, paperback. Adult & teen.
  (ISBN 978-1-882646-10-4)

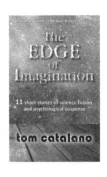

- **Tall Tales & Short Stories**
  Thirteen short stories of suspense, mystery, light romance, and humor. A mix of stories that will make you smile and/or keep you guessing until the end. 176 pgs, paperback.
  Adult & teen. (ISBN 978-1-882646-16-6)

More books on next page!

OTHER BOOKS by Tom Catalano:

- **Rhymes For Teens**
  Rhyming poems that don't take themselves too seriously. Will have pre-teens, teens, (and adults!) smiling and feeling good. Includes: *Wishes For Dishes, Stinky Feet, Me Me Me, I Dreampt I Was You*, and the popular *Phew!* 80 pgs. Pre-teen, teen & adult. (ISBN 978-1-882646-48-7)

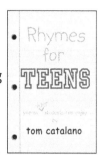

- **Jelly In My Belly**
  Silly, funny, and touching rhyming poems that will have you smiling and laughing. Includes: *How To Make A Friend, Anudder Peanut Butter, Bitter Batter, The Wish List*. 48 pgs. Children & pre-teen. (ISBN 978-1-882646-02-9)

- **Rhymes For Kids!**
  Chock full of silly and feel-good rhyming poems that kids will enjoy. Read them aloud and smile! Includes: *I Wish I Was A Pizza, Bubble Trouble, All God's Critters, Christmas Rap, My Friend Mary-Jean*, and the popular *Cute Little Birdie*. 48 pgs. Children & pre-teen. (ISBN 978-1-882646-05-0)

Order from your favorite bookseller, Amazon.com, and tomcatalano.com

Printed in the USA
CPSIA information can be obtained
at www.ICGtesting.com
LVHW061740071023
760448LV00017B/203